Never Miss *an* Eight Ball Shot Again

RIC COOPER

PAGE PUBLISHING
Conneaut Lake, PA

First originally published by Page Publishing 2023

ISBN 979-8-88654-187-8 (pbk)
ISBN 979-8-88654-199-1 (digital)

Printed in the United States of America

CONTENTS

INTRODUCTION

Have you ever scratched when shooting at the eight ball? I will tell you my procedure to never lose this way again. Would you like to shoot pool better? I will give you my tips on the science of contact aiming. You will also learn extra tools to use on bank shots.

Most pool books do not explain how to play on a barroom coin table. I present new ideas specific to playing eight ball at a bar, new rules about alcohol exemptions, and how to have more fun. I also want to attract more people of all genders.

CHAPTER 1

Why We Like to Play Eight Ball at a Bar

To have fun. To relax and have a good time.

The same reason we go to a bar in the first place.

You also might want to hang out with friends and meet new people. A friendly pool game is an excellent way to do that. So lighten up and try to have fun.

We need more women to start shooting pool again.

For most people to have fun playing pool, they like to feel at ease, not intimidated.

In playing eight ball you get to exercise your brain. Figuring out where to start and how to shoot stimulates your brain and keeps you alert and focused. You can use physics and geometry.

You also will need to exercise your imagination.

Lots of critical winning shots require your vivid imagination—things like seeing a *ghost ball*, being able to imagine mirrors all around the table, and envisioning the shot before shooting. Some people see imaginary lights reflecting the aiming point and the path into the pocket. Throughout this book, you will find many methods that require you to use your imagination. This is exciting and stimulating to your brain and well-being.

Pool should be a sociable, fun game between friends or at least between two or more people who want to play a game and have fun. So don't try to make it a fierce competition. This way coin tables may start to attract more folks of all genders.

If someone likes to shoot pool, they probably already know what ball they want to shoot and how they are going to shoot it. Don't try to tell them what to do. This is annoying and irritating. You want to have fun and meet new people, not make them dislike you. Right? All over a simple game of pool.

I love to play on coin tables. They are found in most bars. They run on quarters. You put from one to four quarters in an adjustable coin slot.

This is usually located at the foot of the table on the left side down under the rail. The owner can adjust how many quarters it takes to play a game.

They represent an investment for the proprietor or the owner in an attempt to provide amusement and make money. Don't try to spot balls or catch the eight ball and start over so as to prolong the game. The owner may decide to remove an unprofitable table and replace the space with a bowling machine. Then what will you do? Either learn to bowl or go somewhere else.

There are some differences when playing on a coin table. Think of it as buying the balls for the game, not as table time. For this owner, the faster you go, the better. It will be the smallest table you will ever get to play eight ball on.

Some people call this a *bar box*. You can make more balls and have more runs.

Long shots are shorter, making it easier to sink them.

This creates excitement and more fun. Nobody likes to miss shots. Playing on a coin table is not like any other pool game table. This makes a big difference, especially in the rules department. Most pool instruction books have instances where balls are spotted, even the eight ball.

On a bar box, you should never spot anything.

The guideline is, "If it goes down or off the table, it stays down." Although coin tables have pockets, they drop down into a *dark hole*. It is almost impossible to see inside this dark hole. That's why I invented the *hole light*. When balls are left in there, you have to put in quarters to buy them back or get the bartender. Usually, they will reimburse you. They don't mind and are very considerate of this. I've never lost any money this way.

At most other pool halls and some upscale bars you usually will not find a bar box. Their tables are bigger and longer. They are usually four by eight or bigger.

It makes all your shots harder, even the break.

This causes you to miss much more often.

It just won't be as much fun.

In spite of the fact that these tables are probably in better condition, cleaner, and better maintained, shots are all more difficult. These tables have leather pockets so that balls can be retrieved and spotted. The owner doesn't care how much time you waste or how long you take to play. As a matter of fact, the longer, the better for him. Just make sure you have a good id.

You probably can't even find a bar box for you to use at home. Even most at-home tables are four by eight or larger. So give your little table the love it deserves. You may not find one anywhere else. Wrap your arms around it, and embrace the fun you have when playing on it. Plus, you get drinks, music, and people around to talk to.

All for just some quarters. Good deal.

These differences alone cause a big gap between bar room rules and standard pool game rules you may read in other books.

These books do not consider the bar life.

That's why they never mention the alcohol exemption rules I established.

As far as I know, there is no book on coin table rules, except this one: chapter 4.

Equipment

House equipment is usually abused.

At least you can still use it for free.

I will discuss different pieces of billiard equipment found in a bar.

The coin tables are amazingly sturdy and hold up very well. Felts don't get torn anymore. The tables are mostly flat. Most people respect and take care of the table. I've never seen damage to any table from people sitting on the rail. You should be allowed to sit on the table and shoot with no feet on the floor if you need to.

Corner pockets

The corner pockets have edges on both sides.

If you make a triangle from the first two diamonds back to the pocket, within this triangle is usually considered the *short rail*. This can be important if playing *call all shots* as well as bank shots.

Some people may dispute this, some may not.

But common sense says this should be a free rail touch. In some places, this area runs a long way out. The tie goes to the shooter, at least in the area near the corner pockets.

For example, what if the ball goes *blah-blah-blah blah-blah* against the sides of the pocket and falls in. Sometimes this happens. What are you gonna do, call two *blahs* or three *blahs* or four or five? And then get argued out of your inning because you didn't call enough *blahs*? Or too many? It takes the fun out of making a ball that you may have thought you'd miss. This does happen sometimes, so give it to the shooter. Why not? This rarely happens at the side pockets. There is no short rail on the sides of the rail next to the side pockets. They have their own unique features to cause you plenty of problems.

Side pockets

Side pockets are a bit bigger than the corner pockets. They are about a half-inch wider. This gives you a slightly larger target. That doesn't mean they are easier. Actually, most people find them much harder. This is because they have sharper edges, which protrude at the corners.

Sometimes people call these tits or titties. They cause multiple problems for the shooter. These shots are often missed. The farther the cue ball and object balls are from a side pocket, the more often you will miss.

If you shoot really soft, I mean really easy, the object ball may fall in sometimes. You want the target ball to roll between the protruded corners and then fall in. That way you can have a chance that it will drop in at the last second.

Balls

They may be cracked and dented, polked and banged, and look pretty dull and rough. They bounce on the rails, on the floor, and even on the walls. Sometimes, they may even bounce off your head. All object balls have a spot on each side with the ball number inside the spot. I call this the *spot view*. This can help you determine the center of the balls when the ball rolls with the spot visible to you. Most people prefer the striped balls. One advantage with stripes is the stripe goes through the middle of the ball, all the way around. This gives you extra aiming confidence in addition to the spot view.

Keep your eyes on the balls. Don't stand directly in front of a shot, especially on the break shot. All cluster shots create kinetic energy inside the cluster. The biggest cluster is the break rack. This is the maximum kinetic power that can be created on a single shot.

This is why you should always be on the lookout when someone is breaking.

So heads up. That is also why, even if you shoot easy on a cluster combination shot, you create a significant amount of kinetic power causing the balls to gain speed and go all over the place.

Mechanical bridge or crutch stick

Most people never use this. I think it's because they are not sure how. This is how.

Be extra careful setting it up. Don't rush and touch or move a ball or anything else.

The bridge end has three shooting grooves.

The center one is the highest. It is used to go over obstacle balls. Unfortunately, it is not very high, so it is not of much use. Do not use this groove on straight shots. It's too high and will cause a miscue. The other two are about the height of the middle of the cue ball.

Use the right side for right English. Use the left side for left English. I almost always use the right side as I am right-handed. You will generally not apply English on a shot like this.

Most do not have a groove when you turn the bridge on its side. Some older ones do.

They will give you a little more height over obstructions, but not much. If you cannot get over obstructions, choose another shot

Or try a one-hand massé if you want.

Place the bridge near where you think it needs to go. Then carefully adjust the placement without disturbing any other balls.

Add your cue stick and continue adjusting the bridge until you are in the proper position to shoot. Be careful and do not rush this step. Then place the bridge on the table and grab it with your empty hand. Hold it tight and be ready to lift it up after you shoot.

A shot to use it on should always be a short, easy shot. It should be under two feet.

It should be easy to tap it in. You may not get a good position after shooting but at least you made the ball and it's still your turn.

The generally accepted way is to hold your elbow at a right angle, parallel to the floor. I could never make this work for me. Now I keep my elbow down and spear right through the cue ball. It seems to work for me. Try whatever works for you. Learning when and how to do this will increase your ball count and extend your innings.

Personal equipment

You can usually get any personal equipment for a lower invest-ment than purchasing equipment for any other strike stick-to-ball sport, like baseball.

Sticks

House sticks are terrible.

Personal sticks are a fine idea and allow you to customize the stick to your style. Having your own stick is one of the most important things for consistent shooting. This is a very valuable benefit.

House sticks will be all of different weights and sizes.

They are never marked anymore so you don't know what you're get-ting. You may never get the same stick again.

Your stick will always be the same weight whenever you take it out of the case. This allows you to make the same shots over and over. This will definitely help you to improve your shooting and inning ball count. Isn't that what you want? So if you are having a problem, a little practice and the same stick will help work it out.

The cue stick will always weigh the same allowing you to work up a solution and then do it over and over, during any game.

Don't be afraid to change sticks or weights of sticks. Some have adjustable weights. I've found these to be difficult to adjust and don't work very well. If you're not getting four or five ball runs after play-ing a while, try a different stick. Also, try a new weight.

I found both my break stick and my shoot stick on a fluke. Now I shoot with an eighteen-ounce weight. I never tried one before because I thought I wouldn't like eighteen ounces.

Turns out it's the best weight for me. After a break-in period, I started consistently getting four and five ball runs.

Beware of people selling sticks at the bar. They may need money or the stick is no good. That's why they are selling it. The stick may be broken or messed up.

Inspect it closely. If it passes, you can usually get a good price and a case may be thrown in as part of the deal.

Remember, the stick is used and old. Don't believe someone who says it's new or quite valuable. If it's so good, why is it being sold in a bar? I would never pay over $30 for a used stick with a case. If it's more, you may as well buy retail.

Powder or resin

They are messy and don't last very long.

The slide you get is inconsistent and will wear off quickly.

You will have to constantly apply more until you just give up and go dry. The cleanup isn't worth it either.

Use a glove instead.

Chalk

Chalk is the worst, most abused piece of house equipment. You will find smashed and busted-up chalk everywhere. There are usually bits and pieces all over the place. Ugh! If not, come back tomorrow.

Carry cases

Single stick cases are the most common. I loved the old, black box-like wooden cases. They would lay flat on a table and had a handle for carrying, like a little suitcase. Alas, you can hardly find one these days.

Two stick cases are the best for the lover of frequent pool playing. You must have at least a break stick and a shooting stick. Plus two stick cases make a great stand to hold up both sticks. You may have more than two sticks. Now there are three, four, and even five stick cases. I saw one with room for three sticks and two backup shafts.

I keep a nice adjustable stick for jump shots and tight places. Sometimes there may be a table or shelf or other obstruction around the playing area. Once a guy put a refrigerator right at the end of the table. We used to open the door and shoot from inside the fridge until it was moved.

An adjustable stick can be set to different lengths.

This may be very helpful and worth the hassles, especially when shooting the eight ball. Remember, that's the final and most important shot. It will win the game for you. You don't want to carelessly mess it up by stroking into some obstruction, table, or refrigerator. You can also use it as a jump stick or to help kids get started.

Outdated equipment

Some things are generally gone. Powder, the break patch, the pillbox, and the score string are no longer found in bars.

Gloves and shooting off the rail.

The latest shooting gloves are similar to batting or golf gloves. They are the best addition to shooting equipment since hands.

You can use your hand to make a V-bridge.

Take your thumb and finger and make a V.

Place your cue stick tip in the V-groove so you can slide it through. Spread your other fingers to raise or lower the aim line and give yourself a solid base. A similar technique can be used to aim the mechanical bridge. Some pros prefer the V-bridge because you can easily see the full table while shooting.

A glove works well with a V-bridge and any rail bridge. When shooting off the rail, I find it helps to grip your stick shaft extra tightly to keep your stroke on your desired aim line as you shoot.

The glove will also help improve your shooting off the rail. Rail shots give everybody trouble. With a tight, sliding glove groove on your griping fingers, you can keep control of the stick from the rail. When you are ready, cut right through the diameter of the cue ball at an angle parallel with how far on the rail you lie. Let the flat land of the table base go from your mind and pretend you are standing on the parallel plane with the angle on the rail. Stand next to the angle you will use to strike the cue ball. Try to imagine shooting through the cue ball as if you are level with the parallel plane of the middle of the cue ball and the rail, not the ground. Then spear right through the diameter of the cue ball, while imagining you are standing in the parallel plane of the shot angle. The secret is to go through the diameter no matter what the angle.

If you can do this, it makes all off the rail shots or any other shot where you have to shoot over interference balls on the table easier to make. It can be approached just like any easy, flat shot shooting directly through the cue ball center at the middle of the ball.

Just pretend you are standing in the same angular relationship with the ball, not the ground.

The problem is you can't go through the cue ball as you will hit the table. That's why I say spear through the cue ball in one swift, strong motion, and then stop the spear after hitting the cue ball.

Once you are set, don't hesitate with this stroke. A quick warm-up stroke will tell you if you are balanced and lets you check the imaginary parallel plane with your stick for the last time before you shoot.

Pool glove sizes come in extra small, small, medium, large, and extra large. The problem is they are hard to find outside a specialty store. You should at least give one a tryout. It can change your game. A glove will eliminate the need to powder your shooting hand and provide you with a consistently smooth, sliding stroke. It also allows you to grab onto the shaft as tight as you want.

Gloves also come in a variety of colors.

Whatever color you like, you may choose from red, blue, pink, purple, and others.

Most are black. Start with black as they are cheaper but still work well. The material varies also. I like the slickest texture which costs a little extra but gives the best sliding and gliding action.

Or you can be like Jeanette Lee and make your own out of a wedding outfit.

Whatever you do, be sure to try one.

It will improve your game.

CHAPTER 2

Making the Eight Ball

The name of the game is eight ball. The eight-ball shot is different from any other shot. It should be the last and final shot for the win. This makes it much more important than any other shot in the game. It should be respected as such. The eight ball is special and more important to the game than any of the other balls.

Else, it would have been called fifteen ball.

The eight ball shot should be approached with care and respect throughout the game. This will help make the fuzzy eight ball not so fuzzy. After all he is a lonely, pocket magnet ball. He is the only ball colored black.

He plays hide and seek with the white cue ball all day and all night long. He wants to be the last ball on the table, legally there. We're lucky to ever make one.

But don't start dancing until the eight ball goes in.

It must be legally pocketed.

Finding the contact point on the dark side of a ball is difficult to pinpoint on all solids. Some people call it the reference point. But it is your aiming contact point and is very important.

Finding the target point on that fuzzy ball gets harder and harder, the farther and farther down the table the eight ball is from the cue ball. The eight ball is like the dark side of the moon. You may never clearly see it.

Also, it is the darkest colored ball and therefore is the hardest ball for the eye to focus on the contact point. I call this *the fuzzy-eight-ball* effect.

The eight ball is always the fuzziest ball on the table, which makes it the hardest ball to see.

That's why it's missed so often. It's even worse when the ball is dirty.

Barroom funk is all over them. A good move when you refresh the colors is to inspect the eight ball. It's always dirty. I like to shine it up a little. You can rub it in on the table brush if they have one available.

No matter how close or easy the shot appears, anything can go wrong at any minute. I have missed lots and lots of easy game-winning shots.

Add a lot more difficulty to the shot when the cue ball is on the rail, even more if the eight ball is on the rail.

These lays may not be makable. Make sure to at least tap the eight ball off the rail, but shoot softly and make extra sure not to scratch.

Never shoot just for the lie. If you have no shot, at least try to improve your position.

Leaving your opponent in a bad place does nothing to help you. Why wait for him to help you? Help yourself. I'm surprised how many people don't try to do this. At least try not to miss touching and tapping the eight ball into a better place. Otherwise, you will have to start all over when your next inning comes up.

You will have to waste another shot to improve your position. Besides, what do you have to lose? Whatever happens, you still have to establish what to shoot next. If you can find a way to try to make the shot, call it but never risk a scratch.

My old system used to be this catchphrase, "Always, always, always take careful aim. Never, never, never, scratch." This was a good start but not enough. If you scratch you lose

So why take a chance and scratch, only to lose the game, even if you make the eight ball?

Now the rule is *one rail only*. If not, that second rail may be a pocket. Why did you have to shoot a duck so hard only to roll as far as to reach another rail?

Especially a rail down at the other end of the table?

I have seen this dozens and dozens of times. That's why I developed my *prevent-the-scratch* procedure.

That is one reason why I wrote this book.

So how can you fully avoid a scratch? Here is my method to never scratch on the eight ball or any ball. The main idea is to position the cue ball after the shot so as not to scratch.

Prevent the scratch

1. Apply more tools to this final shot, if you want to win. Use everything you got.

2. Shoot hard enough to only hit no more than one rail. This is very important. Learning to do this will prevent 85 percent to 95 percent of scratches.

Remember, *only one rail.*

3. If you have good speed control, you sometimes can risk a scratch if the eight ball is closer to the called pocket than the cue ball is from the scratch pocket. You must shoot just hard enough to make the eight ball, yet soft enough to stop the cue ball right in front of the scratch pocket. If it's too risky don't try this. But this is the cure for some of the other 5 percent to 15 percent of the time when you may hit more than one rail. But it only works if the eight ball is somewhat closer to the called pocket than the cue ball is to the scratch pocket. If not, don't try this. It is much easier when the scratch pocket is at the other end of the table. When you do this, it feels pretty fantastic.

4. Making the eight ball is the last shot, so you don't need to worry about positioning the cue ball for the next shot. However, if you determine you are in danger of scratching, try to position the cue ball so as not to scratch. I generally try to leave it safely near the middle of the table. If the risk is great, it's better to prevent a scratch than to make the eight ball and lose anyway. Always access the eight-ball risk of scratching. Most people never do. You may not want to put that much thought and care into every shot.

Maybe you should.

Either way, you should always do this when trying to shoot the eight ball in the called pocket for the win.

Also, take extra care not to scratch on a so-called duck shot, especially if it is slightly inside the pocket.

Do you think it's easy? Yes, it's easy to scratch and lose by following the ball in or by shooting too hard.

Try to *cheat the pocket* or come off the pocket rail to avoid following the object ball. You may also choose to apply heavy English to cause the cue ball to avoid the pocket.

Allow yourself at least some slack to make a mistake. You will probably make a miscue now and then. If you experience too many, slow down and concentrate on your warm-up strokes.

Focus on delivering the stick straight through the cue ball. Be sure to chalk up after every shot. This will help reduce miscues. But don't beat yourself up for either. If it gets to be a problem, reread my book, study, think, and practice as you play until you are satisfied with your game. Just like in life, you cannot be perfect in every game, every day. Make sure not to one-hand, poke, or jerk your stick.

This is legal and is called a one-handed massé. You will almost always miss. Why try it on such an important shot? If it's a short, dangerous stretch, learn to use the mechanical bridge.

By the way, this procedure will avoid any scratch, on any shot. Except for that rare scratch that will happen anyway. This may be caused by unintended English. But usually, it's because you shoot too hard. So if you want to prevent some of the rare scratches, think it through and shoot easier. Also, you will rarely scratch due to chalk or dirt or dust on the table.

Sometimes you may scratch due to dented or chipped balls or a myriad of other reasons. Sometimes you may get something in your eyes; close your eyes, or look away at the wrong moment.

Three-ball plan

Some people say to think several shots ahead or even several games ahead. This is for tournament games or straight pool. In eight-ball games, most people can plan at least three balls ahead. Having a three-ball plan will help you have longer runs. First, choose the shot at hand. Then choose the next ball and try to place the cue ball in the position zone for that ball.

The position zone is an imaginary triangle coming out of the next object ball. The top of the triangle points through the object ball to the center of the target pocket. It then spreads out over the table at about forty-five degrees in front of the ball you are going to shoot next.

When striking the object ball without English the cue ball will rebound at ninety degrees.

Use this right angle to estimate where the cue ball will go after shooting. The third ball is the next one in your plan. You probably won't be able to make the third ball if you don't get the right angle on the second ball.

Most people do not have a preshot routine.

It's time for you to create yours. They can range from three or four steps to over twenty. I find my routine changes depending on the type of shot I am facing. Make your plan during your preshot routine.

Here are my preshot routines.

Bank-shot routine

This takes longer because I add extra steps on a bank shot. See chapter 3 for my banking preshot routine.

General preshot routine for every shot

Start all preshot routines like this.

First, survey the table for your best choice of what you think you can make. Walk around the table and look for interference balls. This is when you try to make your three-ball plan.

Then try to imagine the shot. In your mind see the path the ball will take going into the pocket. I have a hard time envisioning a shot.

Sometimes I will do it twice. It does get easier the longer you play. You may need to level your stick by resting it on the rail. Take your backhand and place that end on the table.

Now, grip lightly and raise the stick slightly.

Now you are near level. This helps a lot.

Chances are, you were holding your stick way off level. Next, determine the need for English if you need to get position for the next shot. Now take your stance. Get your balance. Adjust your stroke and bridge.

Sometimes I take a breath to relax.

See your aim line. Then shoot smoothly through the diameter at the center of the cue ball.

Preshot routine to block distractions

It shouldn't happen, but some loser will always try to distract you. I developed a special preshot routine to be ready to block most distractions. They will commonly ask you a question as you are starting your stroke.

When you are deliberately distracted, take a pause.

Be ready to stop. Stand up straight, and place your stick by your side. This makes you start over. If I know this will happen or if you are on a second or third pause, just pretend you are getting ready to shoot. Listen and look at them. They might say something funny. So take a laugh and start over.

Most likely it will be a question or some smart comment to try to make fun of you. On the third pause, I look at them and say, "Are you done yet?" Even this may not stop them.

When you are shooting the eight ball they might even grab the eight ball and push it in the pocket. Or move it off the target line. This should be an immediate forfeit. No eight-ball shot is easy.

But it is the final shot, so always be extra careful.

Use the procedures in this book to help you win.

No one can *make* you miss. You have to grow out of being distracted. Like Philly Mike said, "Learn to ignore harassment. It makes you a better player." I still don't get it.

You can never eliminate every single scratch, even if I said you could. Sometimes the cue ball will *cling* or stick to the object ball and cause it to skid a few inches going along an improper line instead of going into the pocket. A smudge of chalk or countless other stains will cause a *cling* creating excessive throw. This can also cause an unexpected scratch. But with study, practice, and this book you can keep scratches to your personal bare minimum.

Try to refresh the colors in your mind.

I invented this to help your mind clear the fuzz. Before you start playing, line up the solids and gaze at each one from the yellow one to the black one. If you don't have time to line them all up, at least visually compare the yellow ball to the black. This will focus your mind on the colors and refresh your vision of the surface of the fuzzy eight ball.

CHAPTER 3

Bank Shots, Skill Levels, and English Effects

Bank shots are always difficult. Sometimes that may be the only shot available. It will help if you use all the tools in your pool tool belt. Here are some that work for me.

The golden geometric rule of all bank shots is, "The angle in is equal to the angle out." This will not be true with added intended or unintended English applied. Now other books tell it differently.

They use the triangle method. I like the mirror table method. The problem is every shot and every table is different.

Here is my preshot routine for bank shots.

Start with a survey of the table. I like to hold up my stick like a survey instrument. This will allow you to examine the shot to determine the position of the angle from the object ball to the pocket. Place the stick upright and line it up at the point you see as the middle of the angle between the object ball and the center of the target pocket. This will be your aiming reference point and the contact point of the object ball at the rail. I usually note the distance to or from the nearest diamond. You should not mark the table physically. But mark it in your mind. Then go around the table behind the cue ball and look in the imaginary table mirror, aim through the rail, and shoot at the imaginary pocket in the mirror.

Use your imagination to see a vision of *mirror tables* for almost all bank shots. This concept is very useful as an additional tool in your pool tool belt. I always use it just to make sure my aim is headed in the right direction.

In your mind picture mirrors all around the table. This will help you imagine the mirror in any direction. You simply shoot the ball into the imaginary mirror pocket and watch it go into the target pocket.

In order to shoot my best, I use every method I know and then some. I try to cover all bases even if I don't use them when I shoot.

In the eight-ball game, it's really only critical to use extreme, careful aiming on all eight ball shots.

Playing eight-ball bank or bank the eight

There are cross banks, double-banks, the full table long bank, and many others. There are even two, three, or more rail bank shots that can be made. There is also a bank shot where the cue ball hits the rail first. This is called a kick shot. Willie Mosconi won the world championship title with the famous five rail bank kick shot. All will come up when playing bank the eight. Keep playing this variation until you improve your shooting in all types of bank shots.

This game is really fun to play. You will almost always get a try at the eight ball even if you're way behind. Your opponent will be banking the eight ball, and your balls will be the only ones on the table. Late in the game, you can *walk the dog* and catch up.

Now, can you bank the eight ball? You must call the eight ball shot including the number of rails and the pocket. The called shot must be a bank shot. When you make it you can say, "The bank is open today." For some reason, you get three free scratches when shooting the eight ball, unless you make the eight and scratch.

Then you lose. For me, this is the best way to practice and learn to bank. And it's fun to play.

This game is also fun to watch. Sometimes you will see amazing shots. I like the three-rail bank or a three-rail kick shot. Philly Mike taught me how to do this. You measure the angle at your end of the table into the pocket next to you off the third rail. The second rail doesn't enter into the calculation of the angle back so you don't have to worry about it.

Even when you miss, it's exciting to see it come off the third rail and start heading toward a pocket at the end of the table.

People will usually agree on the *short rail.*

Many shots touch part of the pocket rail, the titties or corners, and drop in. You should not have to call this. They also agree that when a cue ball or target ball hits a rail; it's a bank shot.

Skill levels

First I would like to say there are both men and women in all skill levels. One of the greatest world champions of all time is a young girl from South Korea known as the Black Widow, named Jeanette Lee. She is called the black widow because she is dressed in black. Although I think it may be because she *killed* the great male players.

At only nineteen years old she won her first of many world championship titles. Many of you have seen her on DVD and TV doing trick shots. She's been known to make over two hundred balls per inning.

Skill levels are difficult to judge. You cannot judge a pool player's potential at a glance. True potential lies hidden below the surface. Don't underestimate the importance of mental toughness or the ability to stay focused under pressure. Here are my classifications for skill levels. I use the number of games played and ball count per inning to split the categories. Start at the beginning.

Beginners

Young kids and first-time shooters are beginners. I started shooting pool when my parents gave me and my brothers and sister a bumper pool game for Christmas. It is great for kids to learn to shoot. The table is small. The sticks are smaller. In a game, each opposing side gets only one pocket to shoot at.

Fun lovers

This could be everyone. This group may include players of all skill levels. I like to play with these people. They are usually lots of fun and love to shoot pool. They just want to have fun, no matter how well they shoot.

Good shooters

This is a person who has played maybe over one hundred games. They know how to shoot with accuracy. Two- and three-ball runs are common with them, sometimes even more.

Real good shooters

This person has played over one thousand or more games. They shoot really good. Four, five, and six ball runs are common for them, even more once in a while. That makes it really fun for everyone. These people may draw a crowd to watch them. They are exciting to watch.

You might learn some tips or tricks.

Professional level

These are the real professionals. They will average at least eight to ten balls per inning.

The champions can sink over two hundred balls per inning. They don't really like eight ball.

They think it's too easy. The good news is, professionals seldom, if ever, come into our bars to play pool. They really don't like to play on a coin table. It's too small for them.

My advice is to watch them on TV, enjoy, and try to learn a few things.

Regular people can shoot good pool also.

Anyone can get into the zone and win. When you're hot, you're hot.

To slip into the zone again, try to remember how you got there. See it in your mind, and remember how you felt at the time. This way you can slip into the zone again. There's nothing better when playing pool than to be *in the zone.*

The effects of English

English is probably the most difficult skill to master. It takes a long time to learn the effects your English will put on the balls.

Factors to consider are user-specific, such as the speed of the shot stroke, how far off-center you strike the cue ball, and the distance between the balls and the pocket.

Some of the difficult aspects of English, such as bottom or draw, top or follow, are well known to most players. Most know how to shoot them and when they want to use them.

Others, such as throw, curve, and deflection, are not so predictable. They are much harder to measure. They will affect the target ball path.

Sometimes you can *throw* your target ball around some interference ball or balls and cheat the pocket if you get lucky. Only try this when it is a short distance. It's not easy and may not work, but it may be all you got. At least try to improve your position on the table for your next inning.

Speed and distance vastly affect how much English gets transferred to the target ball. You will almost never need to shoot hard. Ironically, the softer you shoot, the more English is transferred. The wider left or right of the cue ball center also affects the amount of curve from the cue ball transferred onto the object target ball. The softer and farther off the center of the cue ball you shoot, the more throw you will see.

To figure out which way the target object ball will spin, here's a tip. Whichever way you spin the cue ball, the object target ball throws the other way.

Throw must be considered carefully on each English-enhanced shot. The object ball veers to the side on which you hit it. Throw is created when the spin on the cue ball is reversed on the object ball. Move the point of contact in the direction of the throw. Think of it like this: left on cue, the object goes right; right on cue, the object goes left, even if the balls are frozen together. One guideline you can use to estimate the distance the ball is thrown is that the closer and softer you shoot, the greater the effect on the target ball; the harder and farther, the less.

If it is a full table shot, the English starts to wear off about halfway down the table only to leave you receiving unintended English when it gets to your target. It's best not to use much English on long shots.

Each player has their own style of applying English when shooting, depending upon how they shoot. This makes it very hard for anyone to explain to anyone what or how to apply English to a shot. By the way, a good cue stick tip applies English much better. So don't use a house stick and expect much success with English.

You may do it differently. Some people shoot English completely differently than I suggest. They have great success applying English to all types of shots. If you are having problems shooting with English, you might try some of my methods.

Other weird stuff called squirt, curve, transference, running, and reverse English add to your problems.

To be a good shooter, you must learn to apply advanced English to your shot, when needed.

Squirt

This is ball deflection. The cue ball deflects along a line opposite of the English applied. The amount of deflection increases over longer distances.

Curve

The path of the cue ball will curve slightly in the direction of the English applied. It's just a small amount of curve but may be enough to curve around an obstruction. Apply right English to curve right. Aim to just miss the obstruction ball and curve around it in order to strike the target ball.

This works best when the object ball is in a *duck* position.

Transference

You can redirect English from the cue ball by transferring it to object balls or the rail.

This may cause more spin off the rail. It will also cause the object ball to veer in the opposite direction of the English.

Running and reverse English

There are two kinds of off the rail English.

They are opposites. Running English will increase the angle off the rail by about twenty-five to thirty degrees. It will also increase the speed of the cue ball as it bounces off the rail. The cue ball spins in the same direction it will be traveling after contact with the rail. So it will be running after the object ball. Imagine a line down the middle of where the cue ball is located.

Shooting to the right side of the center will create running English. Shooting to the left creates reverse English. With reverse English, the cue ball will be spinning in the opposite direction that it will be traveling after contact with the rail. This will *kill* the cue ball by creating a shorter angle out and slowing the cue ball as it comes off the rail. If you are shooting a longer shot, reverse English turns into running English after hitting two or more rails.

The major shot missing mysterious phenomenon of unintended English almost always causes you to miss on all kinds of shots. Suddenly the ball goes the opposite angle off the rail on a bank shot or curves offline as the cue ball approaches the object ball target, leaving you to wonder, *what just happened?* Yet you can never be an advanced position player without being able to put English on your cue ball, if needed, when you shoot.

However you can do well without it. Just let the speed of your stroke help you get where you can shoot your next shot. If you feel uncertain about how to add English or cannot estimate the effect on the target ball, don't use it. If you feel lucky, you can try your shot anyway. Neutral or no English gives you just a straight-line shot which should allow you to make the ball even if you got nothing to shoot at after.

If you miss, you got nothing after anyway.

You don't even get a shot after. Your inning comes to an end, and you can go sit down without even a chance at trying to improve your position.

Ghost balls

First, line up an imaginary ball directly next to the target ball, pointing straight into the target pocket. If you don't do this step, it may not work very well. Then put the object ball out of your mind. The center of the *ghost* ball will be the aiming point of contact. I like to use an imaginary cue ball. I try to replace the imaginary ball with my cue ball. But you can use any color ball you want. It's just imaginary, but you must be able to see it in your mind's eye. This method works very well on longer shots. It gives you a clearer target from a distance.

Cheat the pocket

Instead of aiming to split the pocket at the middle, *cheat the pocket* you are facing.

Aim into the edge of the pocket, just inside the middle. Treat this new target line as if it were the middle of the pocket. Use my virtual pocket method to find the way to go into the pocket without hitting the corners. Shoot easy as you want the ball to drop inside the pocket after touching the edge.

Diamonds

Diamonds are basically unknown to barroom players. You can use them to measure distances on the table and to mark a spot on the rail.

Use diamonds to estimate the distance the cue ball must travel to enter the position zone for the next shot.

They are also useful for two or three rail bank shots. If you can find a table diamond about halfway between the shot and the shot pocket, usually if you bank off the diamond, it will go in the pocket. Don't forget, the center of the pockets are also diamond spots. So don't bounce off one diamond only to land on another which turns out to be a pocket.

This causes many a scratch.

CHAPTER 4

Rules and New Ideas

The first rule of any pool game is whatever house rules are set up by the proprietor. House rules override all other rules in any pool game. The proprietor owns the establishment and everything in it, including the table. So if you want to play in his bar, you should play by his rules. The good news is most do not set up any special rules. The bad news is that rules were made to be broken. Nobody cares to follow any rules nowadays anyway.

An easy example is jump shots. The owner may not want you to tear up his felt, so they may make jump shots illegal. Now according to actually published rules, some jump shots are legal, some are not. You may never see the proper conditions for a legal jump shot that can be made. I don't like to limit my tools. So you may be able to get away with it provided the shot is very easy.

I believe in following the baseball guidelines that *the tie goes to the shooter*. This goes for any time it is a *your opinion* call. Some are too close to call without an umpire. Just let the shooter keep shooting. They are already at the table. Let him or her shoot pool.

This goes when weird occurrences happen.

Some calls should always go to the player such as simultaneous hits or touches. When balls are so close together you hit both at near the same time. This is such a judgment call that everyone sees it a bit differently, depending on where each is standing. The shooter always thinks he hit his ball first. The opponent always thinks you hit another ball first. The truth is it happens so fast it's too close to call. So it's a tie. The tie goes to the shooter. Let him or her keep shooting. Why not?

This applies to an amazing phenomenon known as *breeze*. Believe it or not, a cue ball can roll past another ball, and the breeze begins to blow causing the other ball to sway a little. It may rock back and forth but doesn't go anywhere. I call this *blowing in the breeze*. Just let it blow and keep shooting. Enjoy yourself and each other instead of trying to deny the breeze.

Exemptions due to drinking

Finally, I believe we all should follow my new rules due to accidentally causing a foul.

I call them "the alcohol exemptions."

Things like falling, dropping, or spilling.

Accidental ball touches. Other touches like those by hand or knocking something over.

No harm, no foul. Maybe a miscue without going anywhere? Was that your shot? You have to roll the ball somewhere on the table to be considered a shot. You get two to six inches of outflow and you can move it back.

But it's not necessary. It's your choice, so shoot and get it over with.

A ball is touched with sticks. Put 'em back.

Break. I guess you break until you like the results. Most people do that already. You are actually in the bar to have a drink.

You're not going to stop drinking just because your shooting pool, are you?

It shouldn't be a problem.

Ironically, most people already give the shooter a pass when some of these happen.

It's like the pool shooters mulligan or do over.

I agree. Why not make a new rule making this legal? This may help bar business and prevent a purest from hassling you when it happens. This would include a sloppy break and touching balls with your stick or hands while shooting.

Most players currently allow this now. But they disagree on whether or not you leave moved balls where they end up or try to move them back as close as possible to where they originally were.

Some people instinctively move it back anyway.

What if balls were moved deliberately yet made to look like an accident? Not fair. So move them back as close as you can so whoever is shooting can keep shooting.

You can never move them back exactly to the same spot, but you can restore the table as close as you can to where it was. The actual rule is that it's up to the opponent to either accept where things are and go ahead with the rest of the inning or ask to have them moved back to near where they were. Common sense says to restore the table back to as close as you can to where it was.

Whatever, the choice goes to the opponent, not the shooter, and not even to an umpire, if you have one. The opponent can choose either and should not be bullied by anyone.

An exception is the eight ball, which is special.

If it is moved while the shooter is getting ready to shoot, it's an immediate forfeit or surrender.

No one, especially a passerby, can touch the eight ball as a shooter begins to shoot it.

Here are some new coin table rules for today's eight-ball games. The old rule, "One foot on the floor" needs to go. Somebody told me in the future we may be living in the *Jetson era*. What this means to me is that someday I may be able to get a jet pack and fly over the table to shoot. This way I won't have to use the mechanical bridge anymore.

The old one foot on the floor rule discriminates against females, short people, superman, and me.

Presenting one of my ideas for new pool playing equipment, the *Peter Pan harness*.

The Peter Pan harness

Each pool hall would install a theatrical harness similar to the one first seen in the stage play *Peter Pan*. You strap yourself in, and your buddy guides you up over the table into position for you to reach a shot that you can't stretch out to reach from the floor. This would eliminate the need for the feared and seldom-used mechanical bridge. It would also end discrimination against women, short people, and even Superman if he stops in to play a game.

I would use it all the time so I could fly around and hover over the table. Can you imagine someone saying, "Hey, one foot on the floor, no flying?"

I'd say, "Oh yeah? Come get me." They're still living in the past.

Other rule updates

If you make the eight ball on the break, you win.

Believe it or not, the rules say you lose. They say you must sink all your stripes or solids first. Bunk.

You don't even have stripes or solids yet. The game is called eight ball, and you must legally sink it.

Well, the break is a legal shot. Just try to take the win away from some lucky person who sinks the eight ball on the break. They get the win.

Another rule that is obsolete is when shooting at the eight ball you must touch it or you lose.

What? You didn't scratch, you just missed a shot.

Why should you lose? Your opponent hasn't earned the win yet and probably doesn't want it that way. In fact this old rule is never called nowadays anyway. Just get rid of it to improve everyone's love of the game.

My new ideas

Divide the table into two squares of three feet by three feet with pockets at every corner.

Try to make all the balls in the square you're in before leaving the square. I call this *cleaning the square*. Leaving the square means shooting or rolling out of the square you are in and going down the table. Be a cleaner. Clean the square before leaving it, if possible. The idea is, shots in the square will be under three feet. Shots down the table will be up to six feet. Short shots are generally easier. But not always. If nothing can be made or you see a shot in another square that will be easy for you to make, take it. Maybe you will have balls to clear in that square. If you can leave the square to make an easy shot, do it.

There is also a third three-foot square in the middle of the table. Just divide the table at the second diamond along both sides of the table, at the head and foot of the table. This is another three-foot square.

The difference is some shots will be into side pockets, and some will be down at the corners. Either way, your balls should be less than three feet apart. Or you can always do whatever you want.

Aim a kick shot backward. Go to the target object ball, and pretend to shoot the object ball at the cue ball. Get your aim line, and spot on the rail for the kick.

Allow for side hits if the space between the pocket corner is tight. Then go back to the cue ball and shoot. The idea is if you can hit it from one ball, you can hit it from the other.

Create a throw measurement tool capable of estimating the speed of the cue ball plus the amount of English applied on the shot and determining the amount of throw produced. The old way is to imagine a triangular zone where an object ball is hit at one end of the table with English and will spread out about one diamond from the pocket through the length of the table. The closer you move to the pocket, the smaller the triangle.

Install stick caddies around the table, as needed. This will prevent sticks from falling to the floor and knocking the tip-off. Replacing tips is expensive and time-consuming. This may also help you keep track of a house stick you may be using.

Press pause

Stop, stand up and set your stick on the floor. This forces you to restart your preshot routine. You can press pause anytime but this is especially useful when being harassed. I am amazed by how many people are unable to stop once they start to shoot. They seem to be in a trance and don't want to be disturbed. They will shoot anyway, even if they are going to miss or should consider another shot. They cannot pause. Even when they are off-balance, they will not stop.

Geospheres

The balls are geometric spheres.

You have to assume they are all exactly the same size and circular shape. Except the cue ball which is sometimes slightly bigger. This is important as the balls will make contact with each other in the middle of the diameter of each ball.

For example, assume the ball sits two inches tall. This means balls will strike each other at a one-inch-tall diameter of each.

This is the contact point between balls.

The spherical aspect means the balls are curved circles along the circumference.

All points on the surface are the same distance from the center of the circle.

This is called the radius.

Virtual pockets

In the past we never had *virtual realities*. Now we do. This concept is one of my favorite new ideas. Right now, no one does this but me. Try it. It will help you determine the correct aim line.

Use your fingers to imagine the pocket aim line. Hold them up, look between them, and adjust them using an imaginary three-dimensional view.

Move them right or left and back and forth to visualize the proper aim line to the center of your target pocket. On side pockets, use the protruded edges as the entryway.

This is very helpful in preventing bumping into the sharp edge on the side pockets accidentally, causing you to miss the shot.

Adjust the virtual view until you can see the clear center of your aim line. Use the outside corners of the corner pockets. Don't forget to do this when the object ball is near the rail. This will help you slide the ball along the rail and into the pocket.

Otherwise, you will cut it too short and hit the rail before you get to the target pocket, causing you to miss the shot.

The science of contact aiming

I have a new way to look at your aim line.

It includes the point you are aiming at, the point on the cue ball that is touched during the stroke, and where the curvatures of the balls meet. This is the spherical point of contact between the balls at each ball's diameter. Focus on a small percentage of the ball's diameter that you are aiming at.

Aim to make contact at a precise target point, not a general one. Try to hit the object ball at one specific point.

The spot you want to hit.

Try to make it bigger and sharper.

Aim for the edge of the ball where you want to make contact.

Aim your cue stick in a rifle-like manner.

1. Aim and adjust the target you are shooting at.
2. Shoot straight through the center of the cue ball.
3. Hit the spherical point of contact on both balls.
4. Add English only if needed, after imagining the complete shot.

The percentage of the ball to allow contact gets smaller on sharper angular cut shots.

In other words, the sharper the angle, the smaller the allowable percentage of the object ball you can make contact with. This happens on the seemingly impossible cut shots that people sometimes make. It starts at say, about seventy-degree angles and goes up to about eighty-degree angles. At ninety degrees, you miss the object ball.

Just remember, the more severe the angle the greater discrepancy between the aim point and the contact point.

The thinner the cut, the more the difference between the aim and contact point. Directly in front of the tip of the cue, imagine you see a black dot (.). This is the contact point on the tip of the stick. When you stroke, you will try to hit this spot. This is the beginning of your aim line. The aim line cue ball contact point is an imaginary spot in the center of the cue ball. Hit the dots, the ball goes in the pocket.

Improved playing experience

Make pool playing more fun. Colored lights are already showing up in game room tables at the malls. Allow beginners to play for free during pool happy hours. Give out a jukebox free play token with each game racked. This will keep the music playing.

Have a ladies' night and a couples' night.

Add a beer discount happy hour while playing pool. Add whatever you can think of to attract and keep more new players. This may cause the coin slot to be set to the max, but it will be worth it.

Over the past decades, when has anything been added to the mix, except for gloves?

Finally, gloves are starting to catch on, I'm happy to say. Gloves will eliminate the resin expense and mess. Why not sell gloves at the pool hall? They are the best. Glove up people; it's the twenty-first century.

Rising, revolving, lighted tables

It would be cool if the table rises up from the floor while rotating and colored lights were flashing, turning, and strobing. That would be a fun ride for anybody. Just make sure to hang on tight to a rail on your way up.

A ball collection tray light (hole light)

Add a little light with an on/off button on the side near the ball retrieval tray. Any player can push the button and clearly see the contents of the collection tray. This way you can easily determine which color ball or balls were made on the break. It would also help to check the tray at the rack to see if any balls are left in the tray. This could cost you some quarters, but let's face it, most of us don't carry around a flashlight. The hole is very dark, and you just can't see clearly into it.

New ideas, new equipment, and specific coin table rules, all will create a more enhanced enjoyment experienced while playing pool. In spite of the fact that some of my ideas seem futuristic, I predict they all will manifest in some form, in the future.

Maybe not the Peter Pan harness or the jet pack, but maybe they will. It is the future. See you there.

The Pool Players' Blues

This is a little poem that may make you smile.

The Pool Players' Blues

Well I woke up this mornin',
Coughin' and yawnin',
Had my pool stick in my hand.

I was lookin' to play,
That very day,
'Cause I'm just a pool shootin' man.

I sleep on the table
So I will be able,
The moment that I awake,

No time to waste,
As I hurry in haste
To practice my eight-ball break.

I was sweepin' the floor,
When walked through the door,
Came a man all battered and bruised.

A bit scruffy lookin',
But I asked him, "What's cookin'?"
Then I saw the holes in his shoes.

He said, "Since I'm here,
Wanna play for a beer?"
'Twas the start of the pool players' blues.

So I bought us a bucket
And said well…what the hey,
He might be the only player that comes in here today.

I thought, *This'll be quick.*
Heck, he ain't got a stick.
I'll soon send him off on his way.

Now, I've paid my dues
And I've sung the blues,
But I'd never heard of the pool players' blues.

I love to play bank it,
So I started to spank it,
As I ran seven balls in a row.

Just put eight in a hole
But wouldn't ya know,
That fuzzy eight ball, I'd blow.

But I didn't mind.
He was so far behind,
I thought that I just wouldn't loose.

Oh, I didn't expect it!
Could I be infected?
With those low-down pool players' blues?

But he just wouldn't miss.
Made a double kiss.
Through balls, with control, he would cruise.

Sure, I can still win,
Then I'll give it to him,
That rottin' ol' pool players' blues.

When he sank the four
My feet hit the floor.
I almost fell out of my shoes.

I knew I was winning,
Just waitin' for my inning,
Still thinking I just couldn't loose.

I started chalkin' my stick.
Thought, *I'll finish this quick*
And then a cold beer I will choose.

Why, he's just a duffer
And I'll make him suffer,
With the pain of the pool players' blues.

When he sank the five,
I thought, I'm still alive,
Then smiled and walked to'ard the table.

This I'll be fun,
Surely he's done,
Why a six-ball run, he's not able.

But the six went in quick.
Then he chalked up his stick
And started to look for the seven.

'Twas froze on the rail.
Then I heard the bell,
Ringing me into pool heaven.

He looked scared to death
As he took a deep breath,
Then smiled like he's walking his dog.

But when it dropped,
My heart almost stopped
And my future appeared in a fog.

As I fell to my knees,
He said, "Budweiser, please."
So I started singing the blues.

I sang the bad news,
Well I'd just been screwed
To the tune of the pool players' blues.

It was such a disgrace,
When I caught a bad case
Of the dirty, rottin', stinkin', low-down, pool players' blues.

At about age twelve, Ric Cooper got a job in a pool hall as a rack boy. The owner was his first mentor. He would teach him how to practice shooting. He got paid in free table time plus tips.

In 1966, he was drafted. His favorite army job was dayroom orderly. Ric would sweep up and then play pool all day. Ric's second mentor was Philly Mike. He liked to teach pool and was a great shot. He explained bank shots and how to use English. His favorite shot was a three-rail bank shot from any direction on the table.

He has discovered many new and different ways to shoot pool. In this book, you will learn to shoot pool better and love pool more. You can beat some of the people some of the time, but you can't beat all the people all the time. He said that.